Read and Play
Cats

by Jim Pipe

Stargazer Books

cat

2

This is a **cat**.

A **cat** is a good pet.

3

legs

4

A cat has four **legs**.

A cat can jump!

5

claws

6

A cat has sharp **claws**.

Claws help a cat to climb.

7

fur

A cat has soft **fur**.

It likes to
be stroked.

9

eyes

A cat has big **eyes**.

A cat sees in the dark.

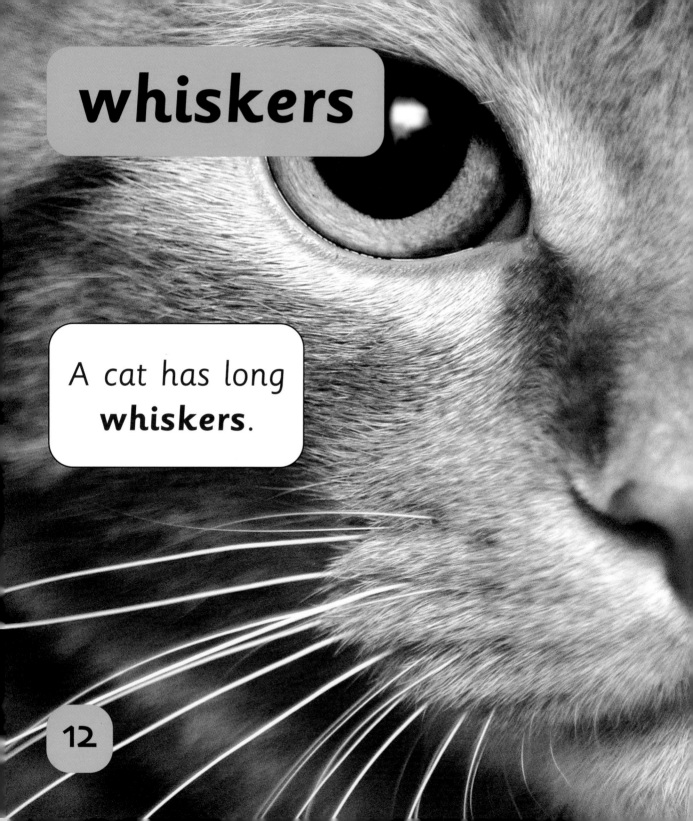

whiskers

A cat has long **whiskers**.

12

It feels with
its **whiskers**.

13

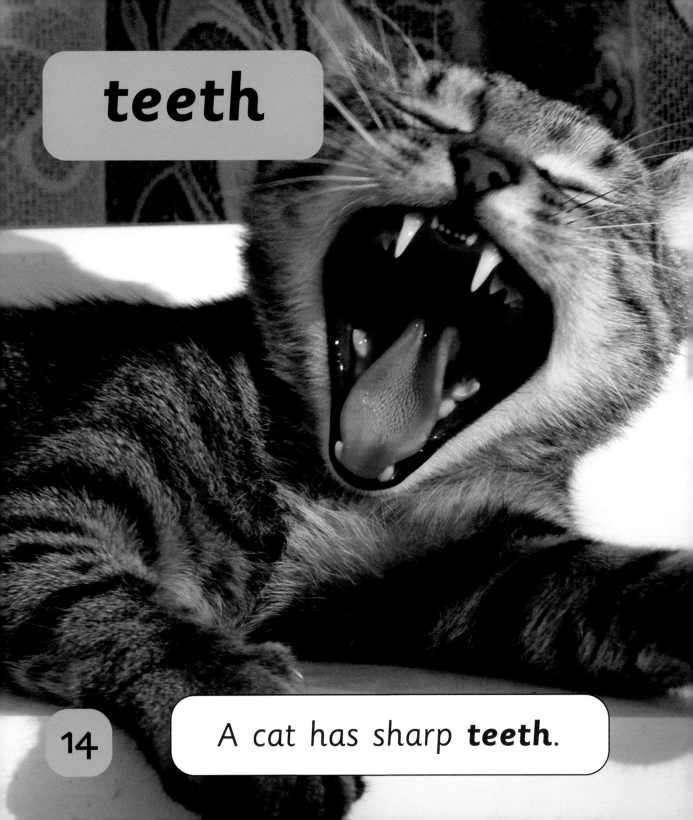

teeth

14 A cat has sharp **teeth**.

A cat eats meat and fish.

15

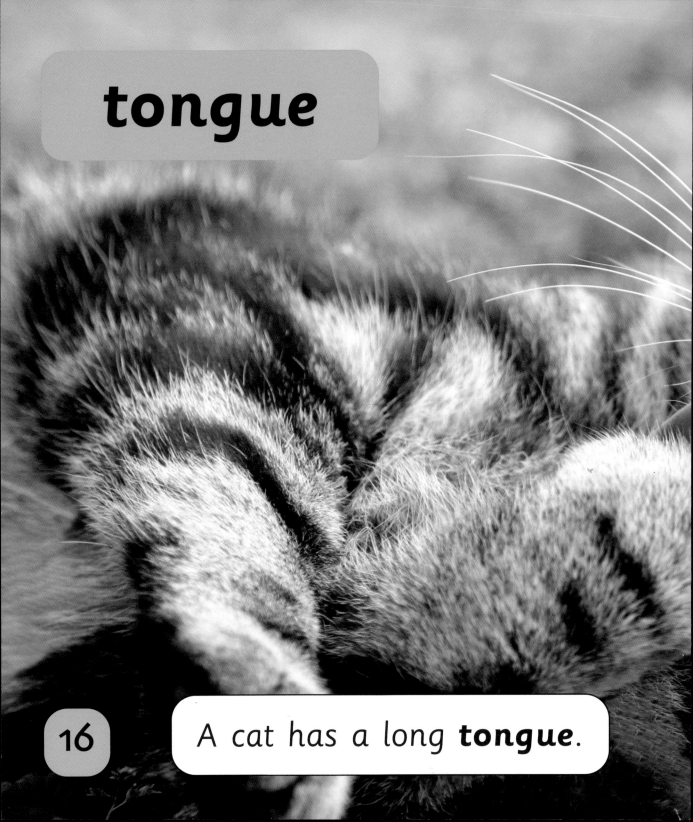

tongue

16 A cat has a long **tongue**.

A cat licks its fur.

kitten

A baby cat is a **kitten**.

Kittens
like to play.

What am I?

teeth

whiskers

claws

legs

20

Match the words and pictures.

How many?

Can you count the cats?

21

What noise?

Hiss!

Miaow!

Purr!

Slurp!

Can you sound like a cat?

Index

Can you find these
cat pictures in
this book?

23

For Parents and Teachers

Questions you could ask:

p. 3 Why is a cat a good pet? e.g. a cat is cuddly, affectionate, and fun to play with. It does not get lonely while we are at school or work.

p. 4 How big is a cat? Ask readers to show how big a cat is using their arms. A domestic cat is about 20 in (50 cm) plus 12-in (30-cm) tail. Explain that "big cats" are much larger, e.g. tigers can reach 10 ft (3 m) long.

p. 5 How fast is a cat? A cat is a real athlete. It can run fast, climb up trees, and jump a long way up or down. Its long tail helps it to balance.

p. 6 What else does a cat use its claws for? A cat's sharp claws help it to hunt mice and birds.

p. 7 What do cats like to do? e.g. exploring, hunting, climbing (cats love high places), staring, meeting other cats, sleeping (cats even dream).

p. 8 What color are cats? Brown, black, orange etc. Look through the book to show the variety.

p. 11 Would you like to see in the dark? Like a cat, you could move around and hunt at night. That's why cats sleep during the day (up to 16 hours!)

p.15 How would you care for a cat? e.g. feeding, cleaning, brushing the coat, litter tray. Cats enjoy milk but it is not good for them. Water is better.

p. 17 Why do cats lick their fur? Cats lick their fur to clean it, using their rough tongue to comb out bits of dirt and dead hair.

Activities you could do:

• Role play—encourage the reader to pretend to be a cat, e.g. walking, licking its paws, cat sounds. You could use face paints to make a child look like a cat, e.g. draw on whiskers.

• Use a raw potato cut with a paw shape to make paw prints. These could be placed on the floor to make a "follow the paw" obstacle course.

• Read aloud cat stories/poems, e.g. *The Owl and the Pussycat, Puss in Boots, The Cat in the Hat.*

• Say cat rhymes such as: "Pussycat, pussycat," "Three Little Kittens," or "Hey, diddle, diddle."

© Aladdin Books Ltd 2008

Designed and produced by
Aladdin Books Ltd

All rights reserved

Printed in the United States

Series consultant
Zoe Stillwell is an experienced preschool teacher.

First published in 2008
in the United States
by Stargazer Books
c/o The Creative Company
123 South Broad Street
P.O. Box 227
Mankato, Minnesota 56002

Photocredits:
l-left, r-right, b-bottom, t-top, c-center, m-middle
All photos on cover and insides from istockphoto.com

Library of Congress Cataloging-in-Publication Data

Pipe, Jim, 1966-
   Cats / by Jim Pipe.
     p. cm. -- (Read and play)
   Includes bibliographical references and Index.
   ISBN 978-1-59604-164-6 (alk. paper)
   1. Cats--Juvenile literature. I. Title.

SF445.7.P56 2007
636.8--dc22

2007007757